NETWORD 1

TEACHING LANGUAGES TO ADULTS

A toolkit for talking
Strategies for independent communication

Duncan Sidwell

Cartoons by Joanne Bond

CɨLT

First published 1993
© 1993 Centre for Information on Language Teaching and Research
ISBN 1 874016 17 8

Cover by Logos Design and Advertising
Printed in Great Britain by Bourne Press Ltd

Published by Centre for Information on Language Teaching and Research, 20 Bedfordbury, Covent Garden, London WC2N 4LB.

Contents

Foreword

No, we don't speak French, but when we're in France we speak our own
language with a foreign intonation.

This notorious image of the English tourist abroad may not be totally obsolete. The fact, however, that it lives more easily in the suburban world of the 1950s and 60s than in the era of single markets and global communication is a reflection of a quite significant change in our national culture. On a grand level this may be described as a reshaping of Britain's place in the world. On a humbler, but probably more real scale it is a result of countless small changes in the behaviour and aspirations of ordinary people.

One such change has indeed been the significant growth in interest in the learning of foreign languages. This should not be overstated - the British still regularly come close to the bottom in most international league tables of language competence. However, there are grounds for considerable optimism. The tourist with his loud voice and foreign intonation may indeed be in terminal decline.

There are undoubtedly many aspects to this changing situation - the requirements of our exporters, the increased mobility of people for both work and recreation, the introduction of languages for all into the school curriculum. But there can be no doubt that one of the key channels for the improvement of language capability has been and continues to be the work of teachers and tutors of adult learners.

CILT started its involvement with the adult language learning field in 1984, with a national conference for modern language tutors in adult education. In 1987 the first NETWORD groups were set up with the support of NETWORD NEWS, a free journal distributed to adult language tutors. The essential nature of this initiative has been one of facilitating self-help groups in a sector of education which has been traditionally under-resourced and where access to training has not always been easy. In the new organisational frameworks established during the rather more hard-nosed 90s the NETWORD network will continue to provide information and support to the whole range of language teachers involved in teaching adults.

The need for networking will be as great as it has ever been. In addition, however, we sense a heightened degree of professionalism among teachers of adults, and a corresponding need for professional training and development. This need underlies the launch of CILT's new NETWORD series, of which this volume is the first example.

It is our intention to make available the advice and experience of experts in the field in a way that will be both palatable and useful to the teacher reading the books on his or her own, and usable by groups as a source of in-service training. For these reasons the books will be essentially practical and will contain a great deal of concrete advice and exemplar material. We hope, however, that they will be more than simply 'tips for teachers', useful as such material may be. It is also our aim to provide you with a basis for reflection about the work which you do often in quite difficult and highly unreflective circumstances. For in the last analysis it is only when teachers (and for that matter learners) understand the processes in which they are involved that we can be really sure of continuing and long-term success.

This then is the goal that we have set ourselves. We hope that you will become involved in this process - firstly by using the book in your work, secondly by engaging with us in the discussion on how best to develop the language capability of the adult population. In this respect where better to start than your local NETWORD group.

The author of this first volume, Duncan Sidwell, has long experience of the adult sector. A founder member of NETWORD, he is a dedicated teacher, trainer and materials writer, with a particular interest in language teaching methodology and in the training of adult tutors. This distillation of Duncan's practical experience combined with his profound understanding of the teaching and learning process should provide both experienced and less experienced teachers with the skills and ideas needed to turn the 'foreign intonation' of our opening quotation into real and meaningful speech.

Lid King
July 1993

Introduction

As its title suggests, this book is a collection of practical ideas whose purpose is to assist tutors in creating communicative activities for their students. For almost all students the point of studying a language is to be able to speak it, and unless they are helped in their efforts to communicate in lessons, they will not progress towards that goal. However, while they need constant opportunity to convey information and opinions to each other, the support they get from the tutor should diminish as they become more competent. In this way they also become more independent. This book discusses the general conditions and techniques necessary to achieve this in the communicative classroom.

Well organised communicative activities are liked by students because feedback is immediate, and there is practical evidence that they can do something unaided in the foreign language. For this reason such activities are fundamental to a feeling of success in learning. They are also important because the nature of the activity and the aims of the student coincide; the student is learning with a method which suits him or her. This enhances motivation considerably.

What does the ability to communicate orally do for a student who is learning a foreign language?

Becoming increasingly competent:
★ gives confidence;
★ motivates students;
★ is of practical value;
★ helps students cope with the unexpected;
★ extends their ability to cope with the world around them;
★ enables them to make changes in the world;
★ enables them to make contact with people in a
   meaningful and appropriate manner.

In fact, learning to speak a language helps students to develop in a social sense. Much of our language teaching has ignored this important contribution to our lives that the capacity to speak a foreign language represents.

Communication defined

Chapter 1

Communication is a two-way process. A letter is written to someone, who reads it. A remark is made to someone and is (usually) understood. A gesture is made and elicits a response which may be a grin or a remark. In any such communication two features are present:

1 Firstly, the person who is making the communication chooses the words (or gesture). That is to say, the originator of the communication has a choice in what he or she says or does and how he or she expresses it. **Choice** is therefore one essential feature of communication.

2 Secondly, the receiver of the communication has to pay attention, because he or she does not know what the other person is going to say. So the receiving person is in a state of uncertainty or ignorance, and that is why he or she pays attention and notices. The key point here is that we pay attention in order to be able to find something out. If we knew it already we would not bother. **Unpredictability** is therefore the second feature of communication.

This may seem obvious, but it is something which we often forget or ignore in the language classroom, when activities intended to be communicative can fail to contain these elements.

In the **communicative classroom** an effort is made to ensure that the activities of students include these two features as far as possible. We want our students to be able to cope with the unexpected and the new, and to be able to originate communication. The most effective way they can learn to do this is through practice.

There are many activities that help people learn to communicate, which are not in themselves communicative. For example, students may be asked to say certain things which everyone is aware of beforehand. They are asked to repeat phrases and words, and they read things a number of times in order to continue to study the language long after they have obtained the meaning.

What is communicative - and what is not?

These are essential activities in the process of language learning, but they are only part of the process. Their purpose is in fact to enable the student to communicate better in the long run. In addition to these types of activity, communicating should be included at as many levels as possible in the learning so that students are able to apply language meaningfully and socially. In order to illustrate how communicative activities differentiate themselves from activities that are not communicative (but which may form part of the path to communication), a few examples are given below. The essential element in each case is that the communicative activities give choice to the speaker and have an element of unpredictability for the listener.

A - Not communicative		B - Communicative	
Tutor	**Student**	**Tutor**	**Student**
Diagram on board Cinema / Cathedral / Museum / Town Hall		Diagram on board	
Where is the Town Hall please?	*First on the right.*	*Where is the Town Hall please?*	*First on the right.*
Thank you. (Points to where it is)		*Thank you.* (Marks it on the plan)	

In example A the whole class knows the answer before it is given. They can all see it on the plan on the board. In B the student who is giving the answer decides where the Town Hall is. So the others have to listen to find out. In A the tutor is perhaps checking that the students understand the use of 'on the right' or 'on the left' etc, whereas in B the tutor is genuinely asking for information.

C - Not communicative		D - Communicative	
Tutor	**Student**	**Tutor**	**Student**

Shopping list on board:
  3lb tomatoes
  sardines
  cooking oil
  7lb potatoes
  cabbage
  fruit
  2lb beans
			The students each make up a shopping list.

Here's your shopping list on the board. Would you like to buy something from me?	*I'd like 7lb of potatoes, please.*	*Good morning, can I help you?*	*Yes, I'd like 2lb of tomatoes, please.*

In C the tutor could be checking that students can read the words correctly, or he/she is giving extra visual support as the words are not well known. In D the students are required to respond to a question as one would in a shop. By determining what they will purchase, they are making a choice.

The situation in the following examples is at a leisure centre where someone is conducting a survey to find out why people use it.

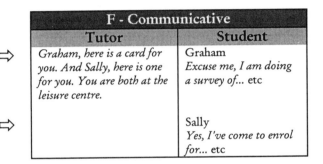

E - Not communicative	
Tutor	**Student**
Graham, could you ask Sally why she is here today? Sally, you've come to enrol for tennis coaching.	Graham *Excuse me, I am doing a survey of... etc* Sally *Yes, I've come to enrol for... etc*

F - Communicative	
Tutor	**Student**
Graham, here is a card for you. And Sally, here is one for you. You are both at the leisure centre.	Graham *Excuse me, I am doing a survey of... etc* Sally *Yes, I've come to enrol for... etc*

The spoken outcomes which arise from the two stimuli are identical, yet the second is communicative, while the first is not. In the second case Graham has no idea what Sally will say. Sally just knows that she is at the leisure centre, and why. She does not know initially that Graham will be asking her why she is there. This example illustrates that the actual content of the exchange need have nothing to do with whether it is a communicative dialogue or not.

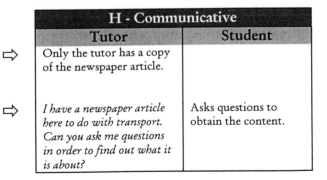

G - Not communicative	
Tutor	**Student**
The tutor and the students have copies of the same newspaper article. *Let's read through the article together... Now, can you tell me what it is about?*	Says what the content is.

H - Communicative	
Tutor	**Student**
Only the tutor has a copy of the newspaper article. *I have a newspaper article here to do with transport. Can you ask me questions in order to find out what it is about?*	Asks questions to obtain the content.

In G the tutor and the students know the content of the article, and the tutor is checking comprehension. This type of activity is frequently used and has an important place in language learning. Depending on the nature of the question and prompts from the tutor, it encourages students to reformulate language; it allows students to see language and thus to absorb and study it; it provides them with a prop for their talking; it involves pronunciation practice; it shows the tutor what students can understand from reading, and so on. In H, on the other hand, the tutor is creating a situation in which the students genuinely have to seek information as a basis for beginning to study a text. This example illustrates how a communicative technique can be used to open up new material.

I - Not communicative	J - Communicative
Tutor	**Tutor**
The tutor briefs the whole class about a journey someone has made, the reasons for it, and the person's feelings about it. The detail is put on a sheet of paper which is given to the students. The tutor then suggests that the students work in pairs, and that one should ask the other all about the journey, the reasons for it, etc.	The tutor briefs the class. They are going to talk about a journey which someone took. The tutor goes over/elicits essential relevant vocabulary which he or she feels the class needs to revise. He or she puts students in pairs and gives the A students a card with some details of the journey and the B students a card indicating things to find out. The cue cards encourage students to add any detail they wish to or ask about more aspects of the journey. Student B has to note down the details.

In example I the tutor has not used the communicative abilities of the students. There is little point in the students actually having a conversation, since they all know about the journey. In the other example the tutor has created a real communicative need and has ensured that the students will have the necessary vocabulary to do the task. He or she has also given space to the students to create new aspects of the task by using their imagination. In order to concentrate the minds of the students who are required to ask questions, the tutor requires them to make notes of the answers.

Examples A to J above illustrate various strategies. In the examples on the right of the page there is an element of unpredictability for the listener and relative degrees of freedom for the speaker to choose language.

Over to you

Task

- Examine some of the activities which you have used recently in class to encourage students to speak. How far can they be described as communicative?
- Take those which you feel are not communicative and see how they could be altered to become so.

Encouraging communication

Chapter 2

There is of course much more to bringing communication about than just doing communicative activities. The relationship created with the students and the general methodology used have an important part to play.

One of the barriers to speaking is nervousness. Students become anxious when performing in public. By creating an easy and accepting atmosphere in the classroom, the tutor can do much to overcome this. There are also management techniques which help. One of these is providing activities to be done in pairs. When they work in pairs students are able to make mistakes without a large audience. In addition, they see that they actually depend upon each other in order to achieve the task and because of this are very willing to assist each other. This adds to the supportive atmosphere in the class. Tutors need to develop the skills of managing and supporting pair work, which involves:

The tutor's relationship with the class

- explaining tasks carefully;
- pitching the tasks at the right level;
- being on hand to help students who are stuck;
- planning the work to ensure it leads to a sense of achievement for learners.

As tutors we all have a theory of language learning. Whether we make it clear to ourselves is another question, but all of us would give reasons for what we do in class. Such reasons should be based on sound methodological principles. The following points are among the more important aspects of methodology.

Aspects of methodology

Clearly defined goals are critical to success. Tutors need to plan their work in terms of **practical outcomes**. Language learning and teaching should be thought of as a practical business, like teaching dance, for example, requiring **demonstration**, **modelling**, **participation** and **independent practice**. Students will want to know what goal they are aiming for and that they can actually do things such as:

CLEARLY DEFINED LEARNING GOALS AND TASKS

★ order a meal;
★ ask for and give directions;
★ talk about their holiday;
★ make a complaint;
★ express an opinion;
★ accurately express their feelings.

In order to feel that they have achieved their goal they must be given the chance to do these things unaided at some point - just reading them out or hearing them is not enough. Taking part in communicative activities and role play enables students to obtain feedback of success in speaking the target language. For this to happen the tutor needs to create 'can do' syllabuses and units of work.

THE USE OF REPETITION

This is an aspect of teaching which goes a long way towards creating confidence. Students need plenty of opportunity to **repeat new key material**. This need is often underestimated by tutors, who are diffident about requiring students to repeat new words and phrases together after the tutor. In fact, considerable repetition is often needed before new words and expressions are acquired. Of course, the new key material should also be brought into subsequent activities as much as possible in order for it to be adequately integrated into the language that is already known.

THE TUTOR'S USE OF THE FOREIGN LANGUAGE

The tutor should create an atmosphere in which it is regarded as natural for the target language to be used as much as possible. By using the target language for classroom management, teaching instructions, giving praise and so on, the tutor greatly helps the learners by providing opportunities for them to:

★ hear the language naturally used for communication;
★ hear similar language repeated frequently;
★ get used to sorting out meanings;
★ attune their ears;
★ gradually acquire models which they themselves can use;
★ realise that you do not need to understand every word to grasp meaning;
★ begin to respond generally in the target language themselves because it is seen as natural to do so.

As the use of the target language is such an important aspect of teaching and learning, it is worthwhile spending some time on it.

• The first skill for the tutor to acquire is to limit his or her language so as to accustom students to a limited range of common utterances.

• As students may at first have difficulty with this, it is important for tutors to ensure that the meanings are clear and that the language used is noted on the board in some cases. In this way students can be helped to build up a comprehensive repertoire of classroom language and tutors are helped to discipline themselves to watch the language they use. Tutors can keep a note of phrases as they introduce them.

• Students can be given the phrases they need to use as the need arises, e.g. asking for clarification, or asking for meanings of words. Such language can be noted down and referred to if the situation arises again.

• Gesture is very helpful in establishing meaning in the early stages. Tutors should, however, gradually lessen the use of gesture so that students concentrate on the voice only, or at least aim for a more natural balance.

• Tutors should avoid constantly translating everything that they say in the target language into the native language, as this accustoms the student to wait for the translation. By carefully building up the receptive and active classroom language of the student, this potentially bad habit can be prevented from taking hold.

One aspect of helping students to talk naturally is to draw their attention to and include in the teaching the 'filler words' which we use in conversation to keep the thing going. Words such as '*Yes*; *I see*; *Really?*; *Oh*; *Mmm*; *I agree*; *Sorry to hear that*; *What was that?*' and so on. These words are discussed later, but they can very naturally be part of the classroom use of the target language and, again, can be noted as they occur (see page 36).

The accurate use of a language depends on the personality as well as on the ability of the learner. Theories of language learning suggest that it is easy for some people to think ahead and convert their intellectual

ACCURACY
AND ERROR
CORRECTION

knowledge of the language into performance, while others find this more difficult. Some people are less bothered by errors and plough on regardless. Still others feel that once they can achieve communication at a level that satisfies them, there is no need to polish it up.

So, the means of achieving accuracy is not the same for all people, and attitudes to its importance vary also. Because this is so subjective and, in class, bound up with other emotions such as 'getting it wrong again' (i.e. being put in a dependent or inferior position), the strategies used by the tutor to encourage accuracy with fluency have to be varied. We have seen that the first essential is that students should have the opportunity to talk in a supportive atmosphere. Ample talk is the first prerequisite. Within this, students should be expected to be as accurate as possible, within **their** terms or capacities, and to achieve this the task set to the student should not be overwhelming. The tutor has to judge carefully the level of the task and, if necessary, give support; this is discussed in detail in Chapter 6 on grading activities.

It must be remembered that in making an utterance students are performing a most complex activity and cannot pay attention to everything at once. An utterance involves:

★   recalling words;
★   recalling phrases;
★   adapting words;
★   adapting phrases;
★   putting things in order;
★   thinking ahead;
★   thinking about what the message is (this can be in
     any form in someone's head, not just in words);
★   trying to achieve intonation;
★   speed of delivery;
★   native language interference;
★   the feelings to do with trying to express something.

Bearing this in mind, the tutor should give opportunity for repetition, be patient and wait, give support, hints and explanation when needed and enable students to hear themselves. This should be done while encouraging longer utterances.

The way in which errors are corrected is also important. Language learners do not make mistakes on purpose; neither, of course, do they make mistakes when they are silent - a frequent strategy for avoiding error. They are likely to remain silent if the work is above their level or if they feel that it is a bad thing to make mistakes because everything should be right first time. It is essential that learners feel able to experiment and to make mistakes, because they learn through this process. In addition to creating an accepting atmosphere, the following points are worth bearing in mind in dealing with errors:

- accept the attempt to communicate rather than halting it;
- use ample examples of the accurate form;
- get students other than the one who made the error to use the correct form in context;
- return to the original student a little later to allow him or her to re-form the utterance having heard more examples of it;
- discuss it, if it is a point of confusion for a number of students.

THE ORGANISATION OF TALK

The class should be organised so that students can talk to each other and so that different groupings are possible. A horseshoe arrangement has many advantages over rows, as it enhances class eye contact and focuses on the tutor. It also creates more equality between the students as it avoids a situation in which some are at the back and others are at the front. A horseshoe arrangement also allows more dialogue between students.

When conducting a largely oral lesson tutors should pattern their interaction with students in ways that are lively and take account of the students' readiness to talk. For example, it is better not to 'go round the class', but to take volunteers first and extend the activity, gradually involving all the class. It is also usually better not to direct a question at an individual student but to address it to a group or the class, and bring in more hesitant or reluctant learners later.

The key to success is to take heed of readiness to talk and arrange matters so that students have opportunities to talk to each other. By arranging for students to talk with each other rather than just with the tutor, the amount of talking in the class is very greatly increased and, with it, student satisfaction. Getting the level right is also very important and more will be said about this in Chapter 6.

OTHER
METHODOLOGICAL
POINTS

Aids to success are:
★   good preparation;
★   a flexible use of grouping;
★   the use of visuals (the OHP is particularly useful because it is so flexible);
★   quick feedback on success to students.

These features all play a part in making the communicative classroom possible and some will be touched upon in later discussion.

Over to you

Task

• Select any one of the points made above about methodology. In planning your next lessons, pay particular attention to that one point and observe how you plan for it and how you monitor its success in the lesson.
• Later, select another or several other points and reflect on your practice in relation to those.

USE OF AUTHENTIC MATERIALS

Introducing material communicatively

Chapter 3

The following examples illustrate:
★ how material can be introduced communicatively;
★ how existing material can easily be altered so that the two elements of communication - choice and unpredictability - can be introduced.

Material can be introduced communicatively or non-communicatively. By involving students and using their contributions in the development of material (sometimes accepting ideas in their mother tongue of course), tutors enable students to take a fuller part in the teaching and learning, thus enhancing motivation and incorporating the collective imagination of the group. This can be done from the most simple to the highest level of learning.

Developing teaching material with the class

Imagine that the class is beginning a unit on talking about past events, and the immediate aim is for students to be able to talk about a holiday. In order for students to experience a wide range of language it is possible to use **invented realities**. You can either talk about someone else's holiday (i.e. *He/she went to...*) or you can ask students to imagine that they themselves went somewhere (e.g. *I went to...*). In the example given below students talk about someone else.

Imagine that the class is a group of French people learning English and that they have some experience of the past tense. The tutor explains that they are going to talk about where Stéphanie went on holiday. There are two ways of proceeding now. Either the tutor:

- **tells** the class where Stéphanie went; or
- **asks** the students to invent and provide the information.

There is more involvement if the class provides the information and in so doing exercises **choice**. What they contribute is also **unpredictable**. They will of course be drawing on previous learning as well as their general life experience in order to contribute. The process of building up the activity could be as follows:

Tutor talk	Student response	Tutor action
Stéphanie took holidays in 1990, 1991 and 1992. Where do you think she went? ↖ *open question*	*student chooses* ↓ *Britain.*	↓ *creates aide mémoire* Writes 'Britain' or 'B' on the board or OHP.
Britain? Yes. Perhaps she went somewhere else? Italy. Or perhaps she went to...?	*Italy? Germany? En Inde?* ↖ *student uses mother tongue*	Writes 'Italy' or 'I'. Writes 'Germany' or 'G'. Writes 'India' or 'In'.
Yes, perhaps she went to India, India. *tutor gives word* ↗ *in the target language*		
(Repeats) So she went to Britain, Italy, Germany or India.		
For how long? *repeated use of verb* ↙	*Two weeks?*	Writes '2 weeks' or '2w'.
Or perhaps she went for... Yes, or perhaps ...? ↙ *tutor seeks more variety*	*Ten days? Three weeks? One week?*	Writes '10 days' or '10d'. Writes '3 weeks' or '3w'. Writes '1 week' or '1w'.
And how did she travel? She travelled by car, by car. Or perhaps ...?	*Car?*	Writes 'car' or
Or perhaps ...?	*By air?*	Writes 'air' or
Or perhaps...? *repeated use of verb* ↓	*By bike?*	Writes 'bike' or
By train. Yes, she could have travelled by train. ↖ *tutor gives correct version*	*In a train?*	Writes 'train' or
uses a 'filler' phrase ↙ *Yes, of course, by boat.*	*And boat.*	Writes 'boat' or

On the board or OHP there is now one of the following visual aids, created by the tutor from the students' responses:

In 1990, 91, 92, she went:	to	Britain **A**
		Italy
		Germany
		India
	for	2 weeks
		10 days
		3 weeks
		1 week
	by	car
		bike
		air
		train
		boat

or

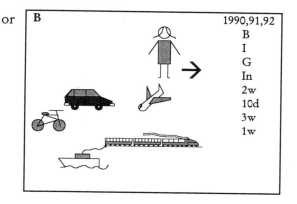

The tutor can now ask the class the **open-ended question** (see page 19), *What did Stéphanie do?*. And the students can respond in a number of ways, i.e. they have **choice** and there is an element of **unpredictability** for listeners, while the tutor can offer any help needed. The classroom activity could therefore continue as follows:

Tutor talk	Student response
What did Stéphanie do in 1991?	*She went to Italy.*
Ah, she went to Italy, did she?	
How long did she go for?	*For three weeks.*
She went for three weeks, I see.	
And how did she travel?	*By air.*
I see. So she travelled by plane. Now I should like you to ask some questions about the other years...	

In this exchange the visual aid B shown above would have been slightly more of a challenge to the students than version A, because it does not have words in it.

Notice that in the process above:
- the tutor creates the material with the students;
- the tutor asks questions which allow choice;
- no-one in the class knows what the answer to the questions will be since there are several choices. In this way unpredictability is built in;
- the tutor repeats key language (e.g. *went*, *travelled*);
- he or she corrects by repeating;
- he or she uses redundant but useful language (e.g. *I see*, *Did she?*);

- he or she invites the students to ask questions as soon as the pattern has been heard.

These activities contain the two basic elements of communication:
★ **choice** for the speaker; and
★ uncertainty or **unpredictability** about the response.

The form adopted in the activity in this example allows many unpredictable utterances and gives lots of practice. No doubt a gradual variation in the question forms would be introduced, e.g. *Did she fly?* or *For very long? For many days?*. Students have the opportunity to vary their responses and to experiment. They could extend the content of the activity easily by asking about other invented people (e.g. *Where did Marc go?*) and add other dates, destinations and activities as they become more confident in the use of the past tense and the vocabulary. The relatively **restricted content** means that they do not have to cope with too much at one time.

Adapting existing teaching material

Material in any unit of work can often easily be extended to allow communication at an early stage.

EXAMPLE 1

A class is doing a unit which practises talking about past events. Let's assume that the material in the course book is presented either as a dialogue or in the narrative form as follows:

Either:

> Last year Jill and Pierre had a holiday in Wales. They went for three weeks to the north coast of Snowdonia. They stayed in bed and breakfast accommodation. They went by train and then hired a car. They went for long walks and visited a number of castles. The food was good and they tried a number of restaurants.

or:

> - What did you do this year Jill?
> - We went to North Wales for three weeks.
> - Did you have a good time?
> - Yes, great. There are some good castles there and Snowdonia is wonderful for long walks. We hired a car too.
> - Is it expensive?
> - Not really. We stayed in bed and breakfast places. The food is good. We found some lovely restaurants.

This material is fairly basic and dull. It does, however, give the learner some constructions and past tenses which are helpful and relevant to the unit being studied. A traditional way of dealing with this material would be to ask questions such as *Where did Jill go this year?*. There is nothing particularly wrong with the question, but it does not require the student to do anything more than read out the answer - which is already known to the rest of the class. A tutor may wish to study these texts briefly in order to provide some support for students who need to refer to the structures and tenses they contain, but in order to give students a wider range of learning, the content could be adapted and developed more communicatively.

If the OHP or board (or a worksheet) is set out as shown below, the learning situation changes greatly. The minimum conditions for communication are now met - the speaker has a choice and the listeners need to pay attention to obtain the information that the speaker will give. The activity could also be done in the third person or altered to an invented reality in which the students respond in the first person.

Holiday in Wales	
Month	June, July, August, September
Length	1 week, 2 weeks, 3 weeks, 10 days
Place	North Wales, Snowdonia, Central Wales, west coast
Accommodation	hotel, B&B, camping, caravan
Transport	bike, car (hired), train, motorbike
Activities	castles, restaurants, walking, swimming, shopping, reading

The tutor can now ask an **open-ended** question such as:

> *Graham, what did you do this summer?*

This open-ended question allows Graham:
★ to choose from a range of possible answers; and in addition
★ to use the past tense.

Such a technique keeps the other students' attention because of the unpredictability of the replies.

The tutor can also:
• ask other students to put questions;

- encourage any student to answer;
- ask all students to make notes of replies;
- then, later, ask for a résumé of where people went on holiday;
- put the students into pairs and ask them to tell each other where they went.

These activities would not be possible with the original material. Students would have far less practice and would need to keep going over the same ground, which would almost certainly induce a feeling of boredom.

EXAMPLE 2

Imagine that as a tutor you would like to deal with different types of dwelling and the local environment. You have some authentic material which includes details of houses, flats and rooms for sale or to let, but the language level is too high. You also have a few town brochures. The question is how to introduce the material in a way that engages the interest of the students from the start in a communicative way. You feel you cannot use the material straight away because it is a little difficult.

So, one way would be to ask them to create descriptions of dwellings together. You could go through the following stages:

Stage 1
Draw the outline of a house on the OHP and then ask questions about it, e.g. *How many bedrooms does it have? Does it have a bathroom or does it have a shower? Is there a dining room and a sitting room? And a garage? Is there a garden?*

This process allows you to:
- introduce new words;
- use the imagination and existing knowledge of the group.

Stage 2
Put a second house on the OHP and go through the same process, but this time encourage students to ask questions, prompting and supplying words as needed.

Stage 3
Do the same with a flat or two.

Stage 4

Now broaden it out to include the location of the dwellings, e.g. *Are they near the town centre? In a village? In a big block? Near a park? On a busy road?*

By now you will have:
- established a wide range of relevant and basic vocabulary;
- given plenty of questioning practice to the class;
- prepared the learners for the authentic materials.

An important aspect of this example is that the tutor really uses the students' imagination and guides their language acquisition. The authentic materials can be approached by discovery learning. If half the students are given cue cards with simple things to find out, they can seek information and note it from the other half. The materials can then be swapped over or the town brochures can be used in the same way. After this the authentic materials can be studied in more detail as a whole-class language study.

A similar technique can be used if you are dealing with television programmes. First establish with the group the range of broadcasts that exist - **they** supply the ideas, some of which they will only be able to convey in the native language. These can be put on the OHP or board.

You can then gradually create an evening's programmes on one channel by using language such as *What's on at 19.00? What time is the news on? When's the soap on?* etc. If the students are then given copies of a page from a newspaper or a TV magazine, or perhaps use a programme printed in a course book, they can work in pairs to find out from each other what's on.

★ ★ ★

Notice that in examples 1 to 3 it is the students who are put in the driving seat and the tutor guides and provides help as needed. The work is structured and the students are led to new learning through talking.

We have seen examples of open-ended questions. What are they exactly? An open-ended question allows the student an element of choice and does not contain too much help. Both open-ended and closed questions

EXAMPLE 3

Open-ended questions

have a place in learning, but the open-ended ones provide more challenge and scope. Here are some examples of both; compare the range of possible answers which these questions would elicit from students.

> John has no breakfast. He gets up, washes and goes to work by bus, arriving at 9 o'clock if the bus is not late or if he has not overslept.

OPEN-ENDED
QUESTIONS

- ♦ Tell me about John's start to the day.
- ♦ What does John do when he leaves home in the morning?
- ♦ Tell me about his journey.
- ♦ Why is he not always on time when arriving at work?
- ♦ What sort of problems can affect his arriving on time?

CLOSED
QUESTIONS

- ♦ Does John eat in the morning?
- ♦ What does he do when he gets up?
- ♦ How does he go to work? Does he go by bus?
- ♦ What time does he usually get to work?
- ♦ Does he ever oversleep?

Over to you

Task 1

- How could the following be converted into a more communicative whole-class activity, and how could it be extended? The purpose is to encourage students to say what they have to eat for breakfast and lunch.
  - ♦ tea
  - ♦ toast
  - ♦ marmalade
  - ♦ salad
  - ♦ chicken
  - ♦ fruit
- List the stages you would go through.

Task 2

- Give some open-ended and some closed questions to go with the information given below.

> After taking a shower and spending a long time getting dressed, Sally usually has egg and bacon for breakfast plus two cups of coffee. She goes to work by car, picking up a friend en route.

> Michael goes to work by car and train. He leaves at 7am and takes the newspaper. He does the crossword on the train.

> He retired in June. In July they went away. They flew to Morocco and then in September they went to Canada to see their daughter. He was not bored at all, much to his surprise.

Techniques for creating communicative activities

Chapter 4

The following techniques help the tutor to create communicative activities:
★ using an information gap;
★ grading the work;
★ using cue cards and symbols.

Information gap

If you know something and I would like to know it, that is an information gap. An example would be if I asked you the time - the 'gap' in my knowledge would be filled by you giving me an answer. The information gap forms the basis for communicative activities. Through this technique students are given tasks which require them to work **together** to find out information from each other. For example, they could be asked:

★ to find out three things they have in common with each other;
★ to find out what each other's morning routines are;
★ to work in pairs to give and seek the information shown on the following cards, while pretending that they are the people shown on the cards. They can make up details and add them to this **invented reality** if they wish.

student ↘

Etudiant A	
Nom	Truffaut
Age	43
Famille	marié(e)
	3 enfants
Profession	ingénieur
etc	

Etudiant B	
Nom	Salan
Age	55
Famille	divorcé(e)
	1 enfant
Profession	avocat
etc	↗

Student A	
Name	Render
Alter	34 *married* ↙
Familie	verheiratet
	3 Kinder
Beruf	Ingenieur
↗ etc	

Student B	
Name	Holz
Alter	36 *divorced* ↙
Familie	geschieden
	1 Kind
Beruf	Rechtsanwalt
etc	↖

lawyer   profession   *lawyer*

Here is another very basic example of an information gap exercise:

Student A	
Departure for Liverpool	*When does the Liverpool train leave?*

Student B		
London	3.25	
Liverpool	3.30	
Leeds	3.36	*At half past three.*

In this example student A has **choice** about how to formulate the question, and **has to listen to the reply** to obtain the information. Student B **chooses** the words he or she will use in answer to the question. A and B need each other to complete the task which has used an information gap to get them to talk to each other. Chapter 5 looks at information gaps in more detail.

Grading activities

A second technique essential in creating successful communicative activities is that of grading. This is necessary to help reduce error in the learning, making the gradient of learning more helpful and thus maintaining motivation. See Chapter 6 for a discussion of grading and the process of increasing student independence.

Grading can take three forms:

Whole-class work moves towards pair work so that the tutor is giving less direct assistance.

1

The materials themselves can be designed so that they provide less and less support to the learner.

2

In the following example one set of cue cards is easier than the other.

Easier version in which linguistic support is given	Harder version with less linguistic support
Etudiant A	**Etudiant A**
Qu'est-ce que votre partenaire a fait hier après-midi?	Activités de votre partenaire hier entre 13.00 et 17.00?
Etudiant B	**Etudiant B**
★ promener le chien ★ faire des courses - livre, jean, chaussures ★ téléphoner à sa sœur ★ repasser des vêtements	

3

The activities can be made more complex, so that learners are required to use more skills. They may have to read documents, listen to a tape and talk to someone before they complete a task.

A communicative task should be introduced at a point at which students can cope with it. In any communicative learning the student progresses from initial understanding to independent performance. This is a gradual process and here we should note that the students will need to practise with some **support** before doing a communicative activity in pairs. There are all sorts of ways in which support can be given initially and then gradually taken away.

Using cue words and symbols

The great art of language teaching is to get students to talk about something without telling them exactly what to say. They can be guided in their speech by symbols and cue words.

Study the following cards which were used in a lesson in which the stimulus for speech was given in the **mother tongue**. The **target language** was Italian.

Student A
What is your name?
What do you do for a living?
Do you live in Bristol?
Do you live far from college?
How do you travel here?
How long does the journey take/do you take?

Student B
My name is ...
I work at ... / My job is ...
I live in ...
Yes/No, I live ... miles ...
I travel/come by/on ...
It takes ... / I take ...

This approach has several **disadvantages**:
★ it increases the use of English in the foreign language classroom;
★ it gives the message that translation is the way to learn to talk;
★ it does not encourage the students to take language directly from their own language store;
★ it may cause interference in the formation of the Italian structures and phrases. The English and Italian language forms are markedly different;
★ it creates a hindrance to the immediacy of perception of meaning;
★ it is likely to restrict the imaginative use of language by the student, who may seek to follow the English. For example, the fourth

question can be expressed by using 'near' instead of 'far'. There are in fact several ways of expressing all of the questions.

The same questions could be stimulated by using a combination of visual symbols and words, as shown below. The tutor does of course have to ensure that the students understand the meaning of the symbols. The conventions can easily be established in class.

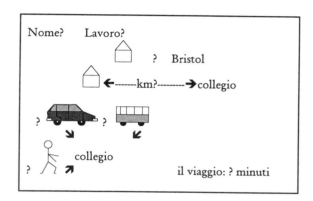

Try for yourself the effect of using cue words and symbols in the following examples. If you run through them either by yourself or with a partner, you will see that you have a wide choice in how you express an idea when cue words are given. Note also the different approach that is adopted when working from symbols rather than from words - and your reaction to it. The cue cards relate to a holiday abroad, in which one student asks the other for certain details.

Task	
Vacances en France	**Holiday in France**
Quand?	When?
Durée?	Length?
Où?	Where?
Transport?	Transport?
Logement?	Accommodation?
Activités?	Activities?

EXAMPLES WITH CUE WORDS		EXAMPLES WITH SYMBOLS	
Etudiant A	Etudiant B	Etudiant A	Etudiant B
juillet 3 semaines région sud-ouest bateau voiture *south west* hôtels pensions excursions repas ← *meals* sites romaines *roman sites*	août 15 jours région nord-ouest omnibus tente *north west* natation cuisine ← *swimming* tennis	juillet 3s romaines	août 15j

Here is a second example about lost property, this time using cue words rather than symbols; the target language is English. Student A asks questions and notes the details which are given by student B.

Try this example with a partner and note the choice of language available to you as you come to ask or answer a question.

You can add another dimension to the dialogue. Student A could be asked to perform the activity as though he or she is bored, lively, curt or expansive. This additional element of **emotional response** to another person, or state of mind, contributes to the range and enjoyment of language use.

Student A
Name?
What?
Where?
When?
Description?
Address?

Student B
Laurent/-ce Ivry
New Street Station (British rail)
Wednesday 9.00-10.00?
blue; cotton; 4 buttons
Windsor Hotel, Nansen Road,
Birmingham - tel: 498741

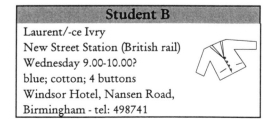

Tutors will need to assist students to use different emotional attitudes in their pair work. It is perhaps easier to start with examples of being curt, as the language used can be cut to its essentials, but in order to portray sympathy, for example, more phrases need to be known. These could be explored with the class and then listed.

For example:
- *That's a shame/pity.*
- *Was it new? It was new, was it?*
- *Mmm/Tttttt/Oh dear.*
- *I hope/Let's hope it turns up/someone finds it.*
- *We'll do our best.*
- *I'm sure it will be found.*

The class can then be asked to practise the dialogue and to use at least two or three of the expressions which should be available on the board/OHP or on paper for students to refer to as necessary. Notice that many of the small expressions we use are not really words at all, but they obviously differ from language to language. Trying to use them adds a great deal of enjoyment and expression and leads to linguistic awareness.

This could be the beginning of looking at how native speakers of the target language convey meaning apart from just using words. Intonation, familiarity, hesitation, gestures, facial expression, etc all convey important messages and, at appropriate points in the learning process, the tutor can introduce these elements. Students need to develop a feel for what is appropriate language and what is not, and some element of experimentation in communicative activities is helpful and can be amusing.

Over to you

Task 1

- Make up symbols or think of cue words to represent the following:
  - mechanic
  - plumber
  - banker
  - sunbathing
  - in the evening
  - ferry
  - cooking
  - shopping
  - how old is he?
  - how much is...?
  - manager
  - policeman
  - postman
  - hotel
  - married
  - museum
  - double room
  - eating
  - where are you going?
  - I don't like eggs
  - shop assistant
  - train driver
  - estate agent
  - football
  - hiking
  - where do you live?
  - shower
  - dancing
  - listening to music
  - I like dogs

Task 2

- List the number of ways there are in English to ask someone to shut the door. Remember there are degrees of politeness and of familiarity, and slang, humour, oblique language, etc. There are many more than ten ways.

Task 3

- Take a simple dialogue in the language that you teach (such as reserving a train seat or asking about items on a menu) and note the different ways of expressing each statement by varying the degree of politeness.

The information gap

Chapter 5

We have seen that the **information gap** creates the minimum conditions for communication to take place, i.e. one person needs to find something out and has the choice of how to put a question, while the other person provides the information in the way he or she wishes to; neither knows exactly what the other will say and so each has to listen to the other. How is this process created by the tutor?

Three types of communicative activity can be identified:

Type 1	Exchanging information, opinion, etc	A ⟶ ⟵ B
Type 2	Assembling information	A ⟶ ⟵ B
Type 3	Checking information etc	A ⟶ ⟵ B

We can analyse some examples:

Exchanging information

Aim:	★ to give students practice in talking about where they live.	**EXAMPLE 1 TYPE 1**
Activity:	★ students work in pairs, giving and seeking information about where they live. Each student has the relevant information on a card as shown below. It is an invented reality.	

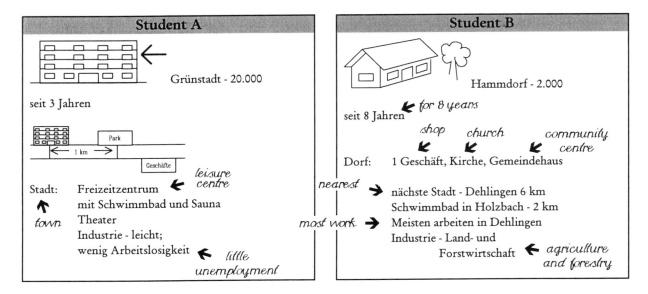

ANALYSIS OF
THE ACTIVITY

What information is provided?
★   Two sets of information about different towns/villages.

How can an information gap be produced?
★   Each partner has different information.

What task can then be set?
★   Students are asked to find out about where the other student lives.
★   Students can be required to note down the information.

What do students need to be able to do in order to complete the task?
★   use language describing a town/village;
★   use appropriate question forms;
★   perhaps seek clarification, repetition, etc.

How are the cue cards designed?
★   Each card has words and diagrams.

The students are **swapping information**. The relationship can be shown like this:

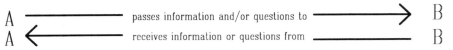

Here are some ideas for topics for communicative activities involving **seeking and giving information**. They can be created for use with students at many levels. The content can be invented or real.

★ routines - at home, at work, at the weekend;
★ what you did on a particular day;
★ what one can do at certain places, including cost of entry etc;
★ plans for the future;
★ family details;
★ the locality in which you live;
★ reporting lost property;
★ describing a picture to another student;
★ asking questions about a picture or a text to build up an idea of the content;
★ questioning someone about an incident of any kind. One student has the questions and the other has the answers, e.g.:
  A *What happened at the chemist?*   **A** *What time was that?*
  B *Well, I was ... etc, etc, when ...*   **B** *About ...*
★ opinions on anything, e.g. advantages/disadvantages; pros/cons of:
  - hotels/camping   - being retired/being at work
  - holidays at home/holidays abroad
  - being a child/being an adult
  and, at a more advanced level, a discussion, giving cue words or ideas for the point of view to be represented.
★ changes in a town or village. One student has the map of how it used to be, the other has one with changes and dates on it.

Over to you

Task

• Devise three communicative activities in which students:
  ◆ exchange information about what they did last weekend;
  ◆ describe their house and garden;
  ◆ find out the prices of clothing from each other (i.e. *What does it cost?*).
• For each activity you will need to make up cue cards.

Assembling information

EXAMPLE 2 TYPE 2	**Aim:**	★	to practise making train enquiries and noting the information.

Activity: ★ students work in pairs; each student has half of the information needed to complete the task.

ANALYSIS OF THE ACTIVITY

What information is provided?
★   A timetable as follows:

Départ	Destination	Arrivée
14.44	Paris	16.47
15.02	Orléans	17.20
15.17	Nantes	16.56
15.39	Lyon	17.12

How can an information gap be produced?
★   Divide the timetable into two parts as shown below:

Etudiant A				Etudiant B		
Départ	Destination	Arrivée		Départ	Destination	Arrivée
?	Paris	16.47		14.44	Paris	?
15.02	Orléans	?		?	Orléans	17.20
?	Nantes	16.56		15.17	Nantes	?
15.39	Lyon	?		?	Lyon	17.12

The information which student A has is not on the card of student B, and vice-versa. Note that where there is a question mark on one, there is information on the other. To obtain the information, students will have to ask questions such as:

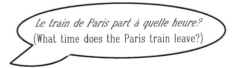

Le train de Paris part à quelle heure?
(What time does the Paris train leave?)

What task can be set?
★   Complete the timetable by asking the times of departure and arrival.

The relationship of the students to the task can be shown like this:

Both students are contributing to finding a solution. They are putting information together.

Notice that although this activity does demand genuine communication in order to be completed, it is not realistic in the sense of being the sort of conversation two people would have. Its purpose is purely linguistic. It allows students to practise certain simple language and is designed primarily for that purpose, which it fulfils well. Examples are given below of more extensive activities which are both communicative and realistic.

What do students need to be able to do in order to complete the task?
★ use appropriate question forms;
★ understand and use times.

How are the cards designed?
★ See above. Note that the cards could be made more difficult by dividing the destinations as well, in which case the students would have to ask:

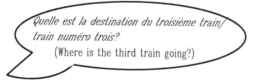

Quelle est la destination du troisième train/ train numéro trois?
(Where is the third train going?)

This is a simple example of how the linguistic level of the task can be slightly raised. The whole activity, however, could be made more complex, while still remaining fundamentally of the same form. For example, students could be required to plan a journey, for which each student would have information such as timetables, tourist information, prices and maps. The activity could be conducted as though over the phone, so that students cannot look at the information which the other has. The task would then be to plan a day out, and certain constraints could be added such as 'Student A cannot leave before 9:30 and student B wants to be back before 6.00pm'. A similar activity can be designed for planning a night out.

Over to you

Task

- Make a communicative activity using the following bus timetable by dividing the information between two students.

	Express	Normal
Twyford	10.10	13.20
Wytcherley	10.30	13.40
Highchurch	-	13.46
Overden	10.40	13.54
Burrough	-	14.10
Swanley	-	14.17
Athton	11.05	14.28
Hereford	11.16	14.39

EXAMPLE 3
TYPE 2

Aim: ★ to practise negotiating where and when to meet in Italian.

Activity: ★ this is a more complex example of assembling information. Students have to take the role of business people using the telephone. The relevant information is given on cue cards in Italian.

Student A	Student B
Si chiama Signor/a Manetti. È all'albergo Porta Verde. Vorrebbe prendere un appuntamento con la Signor/a Gobetti. Le possibilità per Lei sono: mercoledì 14.00 - 16.00 giovedì 18.00 - 20.00 venerdì tutta la serata Non ha la macchina - c'è l'autobus?	Si chiama Signor/a Gobetti. Aspetta una telefonata da un uomo/una donna d'affari. Le possibilità per Lei per un appuntamento sono: mercoledì 15.30 - 18.00 giovedì 18.00 - 19.00 venerdì 19.00 - 21.00 Suggerisce lougo d'incontro davanti al municipio. Le possibilità di trasporto: • stazione metropolitana - davanti al Museo d'Arte • autobus - linee 10 e 12 vicino all'albergo

Student A is required to phone from Hotel Porta Verde and make an appointment to meet Signor/a Gobetti. Student A can only manage Wednesday (2-4pm), Thursday evening (6-8pm) or Friday evening (any time) and has no car. Bus?

Student B is required to respond to telephone call and is available for a meeting Wednesday (3.30-6pm), Thursday (6-7pm) or Friday (7-9pm). Student B suggests meeting at Town Hall and informs that the nearest tube station is the Art Gallery and buses 10 and 12 go near hotel.

What is the situation and what is the task?

ANALYSIS OF THE ACTIVITY

★ Two business people make an arrangement to meet. The students find a solution **together** and the relationship can be shown like this:

The task could include noting down the information about times, places, etc.

How can an information gap be created?

★ The students need to talk in order to agree a time and place. This is a negotiation which has been deliberately complicated by the addition of **constraints**:
- each speaker can only manage certain times;
- the visitor has no car and so needs to know how to travel in the town.

What do the students need to be able to do in order to complete the task?

Students will need a range of **conversational skills** to complete this **realistic** task successfully. These skills are additional to the purely linguistic ones. Students will need to:

★ start the conversation appropriately;
★ know the appropriate forms of address;
★ introduce themselves;
★ explain what they want;
★ negotiate;
★ perhaps seek clarification;
★ convey information and check it has been understood;
★ use strategies to keep the conversation going;
★ close the conversation appropriately.

These skills can be developed gradually with the tutor's help, but only if students are given adequate time to practise relevant activities. Planning by the tutor should include an analysis of what students will need for such tasks, and opportunities for them to practise. The sort of expressions needed in this example could include some of the following (given here in English):

★ Introducing
   Hallo, It's..., How are you?, When did you arrive?, What was the journey like?, Did you have a good journey?, How long are you here for?, Where are you staying?, etc.
★ Explaining
   Can we arrange...?, Would it be possible...?, I'd like..., etc.
★ Negotiating
   Could you...?, Sorry, I..., No, not possible... because..., I'm afraid..., etc.
★ Seeking clarification
   Did you say...?, I see..., Is that...?, etc.
★ Checking
   Is that all right?, Would that do?, OK?, etc.
★ Helping the conversation along
   OK, Fine, Yes, Mmm, Of course, etc.
★ Closing
   I'll see you on..., I'll look forward to seeing you..., Till... then, Goodbye, etc.

Even the simplest of communicative activities can include some of these **discourse features**. For example, we can ask the time of a train by saying:

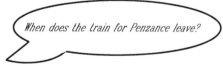

When does the train for Penzance leave?

Or we can learn to say:

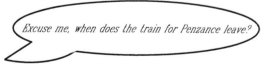

Excuse me, when does the train for Penzance leave?

Excuse me is an example of a discourse feature which can come in handy in many situations, of course, and there are others such as *OK, Just a moment please, Fine, Naturally, Please, Really?*, etc.

These have to be learned and practised by students and one way of doing this is to include a few on the cue cards, encouraging students to use them as they feel appropriate. This depends, of course, on the degree of support that you wish to give students in their pair work. A communicative activity is a learning process and, as students have a great deal to manage in such exchanges, you may feel that a degree of graded support is needed. The discourse features are however very important, since they change even the most simple activities from being purely exchanges of information or opinion in basic language to **social exchanges**, which begin to relate more fully to the cultural context of the language being studied and, of course, to more complex **psychological relationships** between speakers.

Here are some further examples of activities which combine information and which can be developed at various levels of difficulty:

IDEAS FOR THIS PATTERN OF ACTIVITY

Finding solutions or answering a need:
- ★ negotiating what to do for an evening or a day:
  - each partner has a 'What's on' list for the locality; the lists can contain different but not conflicting information.
- ★ where to go on holiday:
  - each has complementary information.
- ★ what to take on holiday:
  - this requires the participants to discuss and reach agreement about what activities they may undertake.
- ★ planning what to do in a new house:
  - e.g. repairs, decoration of the various rooms;
  - the language involved includes: *Shall we...?, Let's..., What about...?, The ... needs/has got to be...*, etc.
- ★ planning menus for a short holiday, a camp, week-end away, etc.
- ★ arranging to meet:
  - this can be developed in many ways following the example in Italian given above.
- ★ seeking hotel accommodation:
  - one participant has the hotel details while the other has requirements, which can be complex, e.g. has a dog, has a disability, etc.
- ★ seeking permanent accommodation:
  - one partner has information while the other asks questions, e.g. ringing up about a flat, a house or a room; where it is, local transport, how much it is, bills included, heating, when to see it, etc.
- ★ seeking and providing information at an information office:

- e.g. excursions (times, costs, details of places to be visited, meals en route, amenities in the locality, etc).

Splitting information using:
★ timetables of any sort.
★ menus.
★ lists, the material for which will be selected according to the relevance of content and appropriateness of level. These lists can be presented as symbols or words, e.g.:

> What's in the box?
> A. *There's a golf ball in the box.*
> B. *And a tennis ball. What else?*
> A. *There's a pen and a ... etc.*
> B. *What's the ... like?*
> A. *It's blue and it's plastic. What about the ...?*

★ prices and items.
★ descriptions of anything or anybody.
★ life histories, e.g.:

> A. *What did she do in 1931?*
> B. *She flew alone from Canberra to ... etc.*

★ town maps. Each has a simple, incomplete map. What is on one is not on the other, although blank spaces may be drawn in. Each has a list of places to ask for, which are on the other student's map. All the directions start from the same spot on both maps, e.g.:

> A. *Where's the cinema?*
> B. *Go straight ahead, and take the ... etc.*

★ changes in a town or village. Each student has a map with the changes marked but the dates are divided between them, e.g.:

> A. *When was the library built?*
> B. *1922. And the swimming pool?*
> A. *That was 1956.*

★ 'What's on this week'. Students have information which they have to put together in the form of an information sheet, e.g. cinema, theatre, sport, concerts, etc.
★ as in the previous example, but this time students create an information sheet about activities in a particular locality, e.g. riding, sailing, tennis, walking, etc.

Over to you

Task	
	• Devise two communicative activities of Type 2 in which students:
	◆ put together a programme of activities for the weekend;
	◆ make suggestions for meals for the weekend.
	• For both of these activities write out all the information (or use symbols), dividing it in the same way as shown in the train timetable on page 32.

Checking information

EXAMPLE 4
TYPE 3

Aim: ★ to practise checking facts or attitudes with another student.

Activity: ★ students work in pairs. One student has the actual information; the other has information which may or may not be correct and requires checking. The relationship between the students can be shown like this:

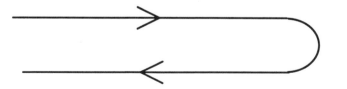

The information gap is created by writing a set of information, and then making changes in it. The original information is put on one card and the changed information is put on another. Student A has the correct information. Student B has to check whether the details on his or her card are true, and has to make amendments.

Etudiant A	Etudiant B
La vérité	**Est-ce que c'est vrai?**
Louis Brun	Louis Brun
Age - 57	Age - 47
Date de naissance - 3.1.45	Date de naissance - 3.2.35
Adresse ↖ *date of birth*	Adresse
App 3	App 3
314, rue Fréderic Mistral	314, rue du Mistral
Marseille *for the last*	Marseille
Marié, 2 enfants *five years*	Divorcé, 2 enfants
Profession - technicien médical ↙	Profession - technicien médical
Clinique de Notre Dame depuis 5 ans	Clinique de la Sainte Vierge depuis
Voiture - Peugeot 405 - 67 84 92	5 ans
↖ *car*	Voiture - Peugeot 405 - 67 83 92

This form of communicative activity requires students to use questions and gives them the opportunity to experiment with a variety of forms. Tutors will need to teach or revise the different forms of questions before the activity is attempted. The technique merely requires any sort of information that can be checked.

IDEAS FOR THIS PATTERN OF ACTIVITY

★   facts about places:
  -   towns, villages, houses, flats, etc.
★   events:
  -   crimes, social events (sporting, outings, etc), journey, holidays, 'What's on' brochures, etc.
★   things:
  -   cars (*Is it...?, Has it got ...?*), gardens, personal possessions, contents of a handbag, lost property (what, when, where, description).
★   figures:
  -   timetables, prices, timing of events, days, dates, detail of historical events, biographies, etc.

Over to you

Tasks	• Devise communicative activities of the three different types described in this chapter, using the information given below. Make the cards and write out the instructions, or make similar cue cards to suit your own class. Use 'invented reality'.
	Remember to divide the information in the appropriate way in order to create the information gap.
Type 1 Swapping	♦ Information - details about daily routines.
	♦ Information - details about 'your' family and their hobbies.
	♦ Information - the price of items of clothing.
Type 2 Putting together	♦ Information:

Destination	Departure	Arrival
Manchester	12.20	14.50
Birmingham	12.26	12.44
Oxford	12.45	13.37
Bath	12.56	14.28

♦ Information - a shopping list.
♦ Information - A telephones B to meet to go to the cinema. Try putting in some constraints, e.g. transport problem, need to get back for babysitter or before a certain time, etc.

Type 3
Checking

♦   Information:

Flight	Departure	Arrival
		local time
TWA 453	13.30	18.10
BA 129	14.45	16.05
LH 444	15.30	19.25
TPA 609	16.50	20.45

♦   Information - details of a town for a brochure.

● Now analyse the activities:
  ♦ What opportunity do they give for practice?
  ♦ What do students need to be able to do in order to complete them successfully?
  ♦ What discourse features would assist the students?
  ♦ What instructions would you give the class?
● Now try the activities out with a colleague or a friend.

Grading teaching and learning

Chapter 6

The tutor has to find a balance between supporting students and letting them experiment without getting lost. Tutors need to know when to let go, how to recede into the background as the students become more confident, and when to hand over control of the learning process to them.

The following diagram shows that the tutor makes possible the growth in learner autonomy by lessening his or her own dominance of the learning process as each unit of work proceeds.

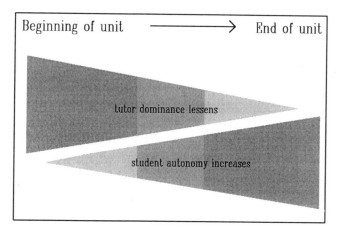

Encouraging student independence

Another way of looking at the process of learning is to see the student as progressing through three stages, from **observer** to **participant** to **independent user**.

Stage 1 - OBSERVER
The student sees, hears and **engages his or her attention.**
Stage 2 - PARTICIPANT
The student **begins to use language** either silently or aloud.
Stage 3 - INDEPENDENT USER
The student moves into various levels of **independent linguistic behaviour.**

We often prolong the first stage unnecessarily, preventing students from moving quickly into using the language, and the second stage can frequently become the final one in the process, with no opportunity being offered to students for the creative use of what has been practised. In any unit of learning, whether big or small, the tutor should always move with the students into the stages of participation and creativity as soon as they are ready. Two strategies assist this progression:

★ teaching and learning develops from a **whole-class activity to individual practice**; it moves from being **public practice to private practice**;

★ the materials themselves are **graded** so that they gradually **offer less support** to the student.

The student's need is to integrate **new** language with his or her **already known** language. The process can be shown like this:

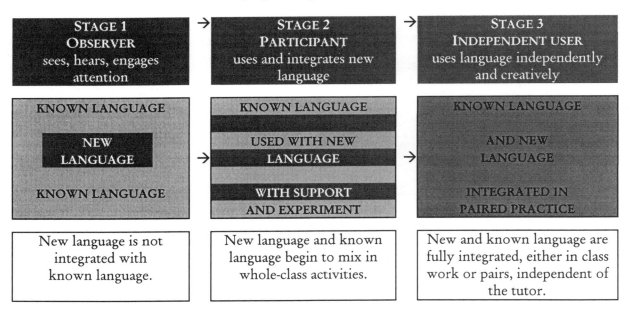

STAGE 1 OBSERVER sees, hears, engages attention	STAGE 2 PARTICIPANT uses and integrates new language	STAGE 3 INDEPENDENT USER uses language independently and creatively
KNOWN LANGUAGE NEW LANGUAGE KNOWN LANGUAGE	KNOWN LANGUAGE USED WITH NEW LANGUAGE WITH SUPPORT AND EXPERIMENT	KNOWN LANGUAGE AND NEW LANGUAGE INTEGRATED IN PAIRED PRACTICE
New language is not integrated with known language.	New language and known language begin to mix in whole-class activities.	New and known language are fully integrated, either in class work or pairs, independent of the tutor.

All three stages are necessary to the learner, but as has been said, classroom practice often stops before stage three, or moves into stage three without giving students full practice in stage two. The effect of insufficient practice in stage two is to frustrate the learners when they try to use language which they have not had an adequate opportunity to integrate into their existing language repertoire. It cannot be overstressed how important stage two is.

The examples below show how the process can be managed. Visuals are a useful tool but, as not all material can be made visual, ideas are given later for using other techniques.

Using visual material

				EXAMPLE 1

Aim: ★ to talk about where people live and express a range of opinion about the area or town.

Target group: ★ learners of English.

The class knows some of the vocabulary. New vocabulary can be brought in gradually. The following material can be presented on an OHP or on a photocopied sheet.

Address	Dwelling	Location	Area	Opinion

number   1-300
Road/Avenue/Drive
  Hawthorne
  Belmont
  Grange
  Melrose
  Queens
  Hills
  Wycliffe
Town/village
  Swansea
  Tonbridge
  Carlisle
  Aberdeen
  Littlestone
  Inchley
		← km ? →		too...
				very...
				not enough...
				lots of...
				no...
				opportunity for...
				qualities
				    nice
				    noisy
				    near
				facilities

From this framework it is possible to derive many original conversations and the tutor can guide and help students in an activity involving the whole class. The elements of choice and unpredictability for listeners are there, provided the tutor proceeds in the following way. The class in this example takes place in Germany.

Tutor	Students
question to whole class → Where does Geoff live? Horst? ← *Horst wants to try* →	*Ah...*
tutor assists Horst → What is his address? The road or avenue? In...? London?	*Hmm... Queen's Avenue.* *No... in Carlisle* ← *student chooses* (pronounced Carlizel)
correct version given three times → In Carlisle. Carlisle. He lives in Carlisle. Where? ← *asks for repetition* Yes. So he lives at 126? 48? *indirectly*	← *student tries* *Carlisle* ← *correct* (Brigitte) 203 *pronunciation*
tutor repeats it all again → OK, he lives at number 203, Queen's Avenue, Carlisle.	← *student chooses* *He has a little house.*
question to whole class → And what sort of house does he live in? Yes, Gudrun? A semi-detached or a detached house? (Tutor points) ← *visual support*	*It's a semi-detached house.* ← *copies new language and chooses*
provides meaning and new word → (Semi and detached get written up) Could you all say that?	
practice → Semi... semi Semi-detached *tutor says new words* Detached *several times* Detached ← Semi-detached So, he doesn't live in a detached house, he lives in a semi. A semi-detached house.	*Semi... semi* *Semi-detached* *Detached* *Detached* *Semi-detached* ← *student communicates effectively*
new word supplied → Where is it exactly? No, it is not in the middle. So it is in a suburb. (Points) *provides* Yes, Vorort - suburb. ← *confirmation*	(Karl) *Not in the middle.* Yes. Vorort? ← *asks for exact confirmation of meaning*
asks for resumé → So he lives on the edge of town. (Does sketch/points, 'suburb' gets written up and repeated) Where is the suburb? South? OK. So, can you tell me where he lives?	(Alex) *North.* *He lives at 203, Queens Avenue, Carlisle. In a suburb.*
repeats again → 203, Queens Avenue in a suburb of Carlisle. Yes. What is it like there?	← *student chooses* (Käthe) *Near a big road.*

These activities enable students to progress with confidence through stages one and two.

The tutor:
- lets the students 'create' the person using their own linguistic resources;
- does not 'go round the class' - they contribute as they wish to;
- gives help where needed;
- uses the target language as the medium of teaching;
- adds new words;
- notes the new words;
- repeats the new words;
- gets students to repeat them;
- will soon ask students to put questions.

The students:
★ have a choice about what to say, from the information provided;
★ have a range of ideas available to use;
★ do not know what another student is going to say and therefore need to pay attention - this is the unpredictable aspect;
★ have the benefit of tutor help if needed.

If need be, some words can be added to the visuals on the framework, or help can be given with structures and grammar in grammatically more difficult languages, such as German, where cues such as *in einer... in einem..., am... an einer...* etc can be put before the relevant symbol to give support. Learners have so much to think about that this sort of help is often welcome.

The third stage of the process, once students are able to talk easily and have created a number of fictitious scenarios about where people live and what it is like there, is to give cue cards and ask students to find out where their partner 'lives'. Students themselves can make up cue cards, of course, but the tutor may want to ensure that a specific range of things are practised and in this case will make the cards him or herself. Example of cue cards:

Student A
57, Endsleigh Road, Barnstable

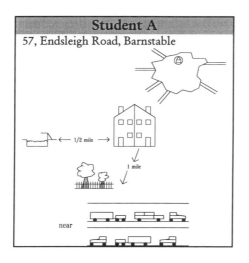

Student B
86, Bradgate Drive, Littleover

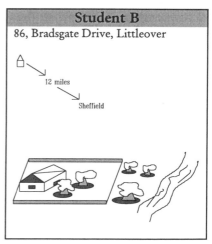

A number of topics can be dealt with in this way. All one has to do is to illustrate or provide cue words under headings such as:

Holidays							
Where	When	How long	Who with	Travel	Activities	Weather	Opinion

Shopping		
Quantities	Items	Shop

Hobbies and pastimes				
What	With whom	Where	How often	Since when

Accident				
Where	Between	Weather	Result	What happened next

Lost property					
Item	Value	Description	Where lost	When	Name of loser

Over to you

Task 1

- Put a list of words and/or illustrations under each of the headings in the examples above.

Task 2	• Do you think there are any particular difficulties connected with the language you teach? • How could you help students to deal with the difficulties you have identified? • How do you strike a balance between fostering fluency and achieving accuracy, especially at stage 3?

For some topics the use of visuals is less appropriate. Two examples are given below in which teaching can move from whole-class teaching to individual practice starting from a text.

Using texts

Aim:	★ to practise making suggestions and proposing alternatives.

EXAMPLE 2

Target group:	★ learners of English.

Imagine that there is a dialogue in a book, in which two people are discussing what to do over the weekend. The tutor could use this as a stimulus to practise similar negotiation, bringing in a wider range of vocabulary, structures and ideas than there are in the original text.

Step 1 • look at the dialogue together; read it to the class; clarify meanings; perhaps ask students to read it aloud.

Step 2 • ask for alternatives to some of the things planned, e.g. if the text has tennis as a suggestion, the class may suggest swimming, or a walk, etc. (The students may need to suggest these in their native language.)

• gradually build up a range of possible activities with the class.

Step 3 • put a weekend planner on the board and fill in the spaces with the help of the class.

• build up the surrounding vocabulary and structures with the class, e.g. *in the morning, before that..., after lunch..., we could..., how about...?, do you like...?, no, it's too ... (far, expensive, late, etc), I'd prefer to ..., that's a good idea.*

Now use this material in a way that allows communication. This could be as follows:

Phrase			Weekend planner	
			Saturday	**Sunday**
How about...	outing	forest		
What about...	swimming	friends		
We could...	shopping	meal		
I'd like/prefer...	theatre	cards		
I don't...	disco	music		
after/before	cinema	TV		
in the afternoon	walk	video		
early	stately home			
Yes/Good idea/OK	tennis			
That's good/Great				

Again, this can be treated as an **invented reality** in which the tutor holds a discussion with the class in order to complete the weekend planner to the right of the lists of cue words (note that the class is learning English and the tutor uses English to build up the whole context).

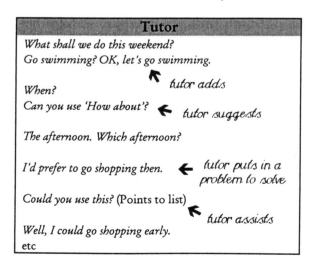

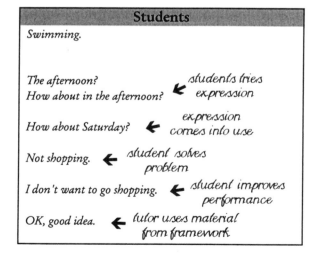

Notice that the tutor:
- uses the material in a way which allows the two crucial elements of communication to be present, i.e. choice and unpredictability;
- enables the class to try phrases, e.g. *How about...* ;

- can then move on and run through a number of possible plans for
  the weekend.

The tutor can note the contributions on the planner and then invite
students to run through the plan together in pairs in order to give them
the opportunity to practise and consolidate negotiating skills. The whole
class can then go through a plan again, with various changes, and when
they feel able, make up their own weekend plans in pairs either using the
material from the board to support them or working from memory, if
they feel confident enough.

Here is a possible cue card for pair work, to be used with the material
still displayed on the board at first and then, later, without that support.

Student A		Student B	
Saturday	**Sunday**	**Saturday**	**Sunday**
9.00		9.00	
12.00		12.00	
3.00		3.00	
6.00		6.00	

EXAMPLE 3

Aim: ★ to practise recounting a traffic incident.

Target group: ★ learners of English.

Students are given the text of a traffic accident, which we can assume is
an account of what someone saw. After looking at a text the following is
written on the board or displayed on the OHP and alternative accounts
can be developed:

Me in town	Weather	Incident
When? Why? Who with?	What?	Where? When? What happened? Why? Afterwards?

For each of the categories, the tutor would need to develop and note the relevant vocabulary, and also the expressions of feeling - *It was awful, I was shocked, I didn't feel too good, It wasn't really serious, fortunately*.

As each incident is built up students should be given the chance to ask each other questions. They then work in pairs to create a narrative which they report to the rest of the class, or prepare to answer questions about their incidents. Alternatively, students can be invited to create their own scenario in pairs, then change partners and question each other about the incident they 'witnessed'.

Using cue cards

Cue cards can be graded in difficulty, so that support to the students gradually diminishes. In preparation for an activity the tutor will decide what linguistic elements the students will learn or practise and which of these are likely to pose particular problems. The cue cards can provide the necessary help as shown in the examples which follow.

EXAMPLE 4

Aim: ★ to practise talking about holidays.

Target group: ★ learners of French, German and English.

A class wants to talk about holidays, i.e. describing where the holiday was, how long, travel details, activities and weather. In order to do this students have to be able to:

★ use the perfect tense and imperfect tenses appropriately (in this case the examples are given in French and German);
★ ask questions;
★ give answers;
★ use the appropriate vocabulary;
★ use a number of structures.

If we assume that they are not very familiar with the perfect and imperfect tenses, they will need some support while they cope with the demands of the vocabulary and structures. The past tenses are complex in the languages in the example, and in this activity the tenses are the key elements for manipulation. It is often the case that learners are unnecessarily burdened with too great a memory load when they are at the stage of practice. The thing they most need is support at the point of difficulty.

The materials shown below can be used as class or paired activities. As **class activities** the cue words and symbols can be put on an OHP or photocopied and used by students working as a whole class to create dialogues, with the tutor helping as needed - as we have seen in earlier examples. Individual work can then be done using cue cards with words on them to help at first, followed by another set of cue cards which largely use symbols. The following examples show this. They also set out verbs, which are not put in any particular order on the cue card so that the learner is required to choose the appropriate ones.

Cue cards for pair work using words and giving help with verbs:

A	B	A	B
Vacances en France juillet 15 jours voiture Midi pension randonnées sites romaines lecture temps magnifique	Vacances en France Paques 8 jours avion Chamonix hôtel ski visite à Genève bon repas après-ski beau temps bonne neige	Ferien in Frankreich Juli 15 Tage Wagen Midi Gasthaus Wanderungen römische Reste Lesen ausgezeichnetes Wetter	Ferien in Frankreich Ostern 8 Tage Flugzeug Chamonix Hotel Skilaufen nach Genf gutes Essen après-ski Wetter - gut Schnee - gut
visité, fait, passé, allé*, logé, pris, était, faisait, voyagé, trouvé *=*verb with être*	visité, fait, passé, allé*, logé, pris, était, faisait, voyagé, trouvé, mangé *=*verb with être*	besucht, übernachtet, genommen, *gefahren, verbracht, gehabt, war, gelesen, gemacht *=*verb with sein*	besucht, übernachtet, *gefahren, genossen, *geflogen, war, *skigelaufen *=*verb with sein*

The task can be made more communicative in order to make greater demands on the student and to give more scope for invention by using symbols instead of words; verbs can be included or not, depending on the needs of the learners.

Cue cards using symbols and giving help with verbs:

A
Vacances en France j f m a m j *J* a s o n d 15 
visité, fait, passé, allé*, logé, pris, était, faisait, voyagé, trouvé

B
Vacances en France Paques 8 Chamonix neige✓✓ ➔Genève 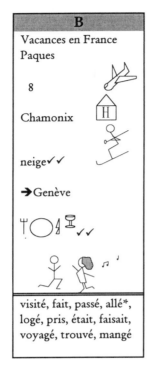
visité, fait, passé, allé*, logé, pris, était, faisait, voyagé, trouvé, mangé

A
Ferien in Frankreich j f m a m j *J* a s o n d 15 
besucht, übernachtet, genommen, *gefahren, verbracht, gehabt, war, gelesen, gemacht

B
Ferien in Frankreich Ostern 8 Chamonix Schnee✓✓ ➔Genf 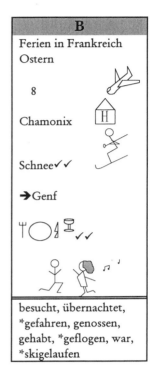
besucht, übernachtet, *gefahren, genossen, gehabt, *geflogen, war, *skigelaufen

The above cue cards contain the following information:

A
Holiday in France
July
15 days
car
Midi
guesthouse
walks
roman sites
reading
wonderful weather
visited, did, spent, went, stayed, was, went on... , travelled, found, read

B
Holiday in France
Easter
8 days
plane
Chamonix
hotel
skiing
visit to Geneva
good food
good weather and good snow
visited, did, spent, went, stayed, was, travelled, ate, had

The final stage in the withdrawal of support for the student is the single cue card shown below. It is up to the students to make up information about the holiday they have had. They are now entirely on their own. The tutor may ask them to note down the information that they obtain from their partner, with the intention of:

★ ensuring close attention to what the partner says;
★ having a report back session in class once the activity is over.

The advantage of a reporting back session is that it practises another structure in a perfectly natural way. The cue card activity is in the first person (*I went to France at Easter*) whereas the report back uses the third person (*He/She went to France at Easter*).

A et B	A und B	A and B
Vacances à l'étranger	**Ferien im Ausland**	**Holidays abroad**
Demandez à votre partenaire où il/elle a passé(e) ses vacances. Répondez aussi à ses questions sur vos vacances.	Wo hat Ihr Partner/Ihre Partnerin die Ferien verbracht? Beantworten Sie auch seine/ihre Fragen über Ihre Ferien.	Where did your partner spend his or her holiday? Answer his or her questions about your holidays.
Points de repère	Stichpunkte	Cues
date	Datum	date
durée	Länge	length
moyen de transport	Transportmittel	transport
région/ville	Stadt/Region	town/region
hébergement	Unterkunft	accommodation
activités	Aktivitäten	activities
temps	Wetter	weather
Autre chose à demander ou à dire?	Haben Sie noch etwas zu sagen oder zu fragen?	Anything else to ask or to say?
NOTEZ LES DETAILS	MACHEN SIE NOTIZEN	NOTE DOWN THE DETAILS

Such material should not be used in isolation, of course. It would help students to read short passages, hear tapes, look at brochures, watch videos about holidays and so on in addition to doing these spoken activities.

There are points to notice about the grading of these materials and the amount of assistance which is given.

First set of cue cards (page 53):
★ words are used as cues;
★ just basic nouns are used;
★ the past participles which are listed are not given in the order in which the students are likely to use them;
★ support is given with auxiliary verbs, i.e. * = verb with *être/sein*.

Second set of cue cards (page 54):
★ symbols are used, requiring the students to search in their store of language for the words they need;
★ symbols allow the students more choice of words than cue words; they can develop their own ways of talking.

Third set of single cue cards (page 55):
★ very little help is given other than what could or should be included by students in their conversations. No grammatical help is given. Students are able to extend their linguistic abilities as far as they wish, and use their imagination to the full.

The progression towards independence in the example is:

from words and **linguistically supportive cues**	→	via symbols with or without linguistic cues	→	to general **instructions with no linguistic assistance**

Over to you

Task

• Make cue cards which could be used **before** the activity shown below and which would:
 ♦ gradually give less support;
 ♦ require students to talk about an invented reality.

Activity
Ask your partner about his/her pastimes:

♦ what	♦ who with
♦ when	♦ where
♦ frequency	♦ since

Assessment

Chapter 7

A most important aspect of general methodology is creating and sustaining motivation and an important part of this is giving students feedback. They can obtain feedback in a number of ways - the achievement of a well defined task being one of them. They may also wish for a more formal recognition of their achievements and this can be given by a periodic assessment of progress. As courses become better defined and more vocationally oriented, such formal recognition assumes greater importance with a corresponding need for both tutors and students to see assessment as an **integral part of learning**, not something that is tacked on to it.

Assessment should enable students to measure their progress in the different forms of language they need in order to communicate. It is helpful for them to have confirmation that they know how to handle a complaint in a foreign language, that they know how to use appropriate forms of address and make suggestions in ways that are acceptable.

Assessment of oral competence can be complex, but there are certain basic principles and concepts which are relatively simple.

Principles of assessment

Students should know what the assessment covers. The aim of the learning should be clear to the students from the beginning of the unit - 'In this unit you will learn how to...' This prepares the students; it gives them a helpful 'mental set'. They know where they are going and where to aim for.

Assessment of speech should be an assessment of oral competence - not of writing, not of reading and not of listening. Assessment tasks should be designed with speaking in mind. It will be necessary, of course, for students to listen in order to respond, and in some cases to read in order to talk about something, but if oral competence is being assessed then that is where the focus should be, and that is what credit should be awarded for.

SUCCESSFUL AND
ACCEPTABLE
COMMUNICATION

The tutor must be clear about what constitutes successful communication. The criterion is usually that the message has been successfully conveyed. This requires judgement, but it should be isolated from other criteria and considered on its own.

A simple example: *I am going to the cinema yesterday*. This example cannot be successful. Does the speaker mean that he or she has been to the cinema already, or that he or she is going tomorrow? There is no way of telling from the statement itself.

Here is another example: *Yesterday we have a very good time. We go out all day to London and have a good food. The evening we go to film. The time was good too, it not raining at all.* Although there are several errors here, they are not such as to make the communication unintelligible. We know that the speaker:

★   had a good time;
★   spent a day in London;
★   ate well;
★   went to the cinema in the evening;
★   enjoyed good weather.

We can therefore say that the communication was **successful** in conveying five items of information. But is it **acceptable**?

A successful communication may or may not be acceptable at the level being studied. The assessor may award more credit for successful communication than for acceptability, because he or she feels that at the **level** at which the student is working, the important thing is that the message is conveyed. On the other hand, the assessment may give greater emphasis to the **quality** of the language. The proportion of marks awarded for success and for acceptability is termed the **weighting**.

At some levels it may be appropriate to award more credit for successful communication, but at higher levels of study it may be reasonable to look more to quality of communication and award a higher proportion of marks for acceptability. At any level bonus points can be awarded to encourage students to aim for quality. This is a delicate balance, however, and at times it may be important not to put too much emphasis on quality, as students may clam up.

The model below illustrates one possible balance between success and acceptability and shows what is meant by weighting.

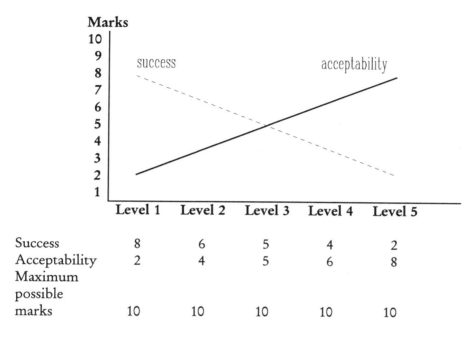

	Level 1	Level 2	Level 3	Level 4	Level 5
Success	8	6	5	4	2
Acceptability	2	4	5	6	8
Maximum possible marks	10	10	10	10	10

In this example of weighting, Level 1 beginners are given most credit for getting the message across (the balance is 8:2); the most advanced students are required to demonstrate good quality to a greater extent (the balance is 2:8), it being taken for granted that they will be able to communicate the message itself at this level of learning. This, it must be emphasised, is only an illustration; the balance could be quite different.

There are many imponderables in assessment. What do we mean by acceptability? Acceptable to whom? And we have to remember that acceptability may influence success: if I am unintentionally rude in my efforts to communicate, the other person may get an unintended underlying message - so I have not been successful. However, the two aspects exist and it is important to consider each of them in oral assessment.

It is also useful to bear this distinction in mind in normal classroom teaching. It helps the tutor and the student concentrate on getting messages across, while at the same time not forgetting the form of the language which carries the message. If you do things the other way about

- emphasise the form and not the communication - you are liable to cause students to become inhibited and tongue-tied.

Carrying out assessments can be time-consuming but there are ways of minimising the problem. In oral assessment the students can work in pairs of roughly equal ability. The tutor assesses the quality and success in communication, including the strategies the students use to make their meaning clear or to seek clarification. The actual assessment material need be no different to the communicative tasks described in this book.

Over to you

Task

- Carry out a short oral assessment in your class at the end of a unit. To do this you will need to:
  - design a cue card suitable to the unit;
  - work out a marking scheme. This should include:
    - a list of what is to be conveyed, e.g. ten items of information about a holiday which the students pretend they have taken, or six items of information about the area where 'they' live;
    - a grid which allows you to tick the items that the students have conveyed;
    - a suitable weighting of additional marks for the quality of the communication;
  - decide how you wish to carry it out. This can be with individual students yourself or you can put students in pairs and note their exchanges.

A checklist of good practice

Chapter 8

In this book we have identified the basic elements of communication and how they may be used from the very beginning of any unit of work to involve students in learning, and we have seen that this can be achieved at the simplest levels.

As teachers of communication skills we need to look at our classroom behaviour to see whether general principles of methodology and particular techniques of enhancing opportunities for communication are being applied and do result in learning outcomes that correspond to our aims and the student's needs.

What are the general principles relating to the communicative classroom?

General principles

- Students need to be able to talk in an **atmosphere** that emphasises the importance of communication, and minimises the inhibitions brought by fear of failure and mistakes.

- There need to be **clear learning goals**, reflected in the planning of activities which are interactive.

- Students need to be given **opportunities for communication**; that is, their activities should include some element of choice for the speaker and unpredictability as far as the listeners are concerned.

- The **target language** should be the medium of teaching as far as possible.

Over to you

Task	• Reflecting on your own classroom teaching consider, in turn, the following aspects which relate to the general principles outlined above.
	  ♦ How do you deal with mistakes?
	  ♦ Do the learning outcomes correspond to your aims and objectives?
	  ♦ Are there sufficient opportunities for interaction?
	  ♦ How far are students involved?
	  ♦ How extensively do you use the target language in your teaching?

Communicative activities

We have seen that the purpose of communicative activities is to enable students to prove to themselves that they can use the language effectively, and that for this to happen the activities need to contain the two elements of **choice** for the speaker and uncertainty or **unpredictability** for the listener. These elements can be built into classroom activity as well as into pair work.

Three basic types of activities can be created, all of which rest on the idea of the **information gap**: activities involving exchanging information, activities involving assembling information and activities involving checking information (see Chapter 5).

Communicative activities can be **graded** in a number of ways, for example words can give way to symbols. Preparatory work can also be graded by using frameworks which give a limited choice, but still enable communication to take place in whole-class activities. Various levels of support, such as grammatical cues, can be given to learners as they progress through stages of **increasing independence** (see Chapter 6).

PREPARING FOR COMMUNICATION

Before students can progress to independent tasks, they need to work with the support of the tutor through activities which give them the basis for developing genuine communication skills.

Communicative activities do not work automatically. If the students are unprepared or the work is at the wrong level, the result will be confusion and frustration. There are a number of strategies to adopt when using communicative techniques:

- Before using an activity, particularly if the idea is new to you, try it out with a colleague or a student. You may discover that it does not work as you anticipated.

- Work out the structures and vocabulary which will be necessary and the discourse features which would be desirable, and incorporate these into the teaching.

- Train the students to use this kind of activity. It may well be that it is new to them and they may not be accustomed to seeking information in a real situation. Language students are often used to having the required answers provided on the board or in the book, rather than being challenged to seek them actively and orally. You will need to take students through examples to enable them to develop their own proficiency.

- Ensure that the task is at the right level. This requires good judgement. If it is too easy it matters less than if it is too hard. A communicative exercise can always be made more complicated, but if students are given an activity which is beyond them, their confidence is undermined and they can become very frustrated. The emotional pay-off is entirely negative and can affect their attitude to communicative activities in general.

Over to you

Task	• Go over the techniques for creating communicative activities based on an information gap, sketching out one each of the three types:
	  ◆ select any subject, e.g. personal identification;
	  ◆ assemble the basic language;
	  ◆ consider whether to use symbols and/or words;
	  ◆ consider discourse features;
	  ◆ consider the need for support devices;
	  ◆ consider the sequencing of activities which will enable students to do the communicative task;
	  ◆ start with a sample example.

Trying it out	• When you try an activity, check systematically how well it went. Begin with the students:
	  ◆ Did they like it?
	  ◆ Did they learn something from it?
	  ◆ Was it at the right level?
	  ◆ Did it give them enough flexibility?
	  ◆ Would they like to repeat the experience?
	  ◆ Have they got ideas for improvement?
	
	• In the light of their comments, reflect on what brought the level of success:
	  ◆ Your way of introducing students to the type of task.
	  ◆ The activities which prepared the students. How were these graded? Did they give opportunity for the elements of communication to be introduced?
	  ◆ The amount of support that the materials gave and how this could be adapted.
	  ◆ How much opportunity to talk each member of the class had both before and during the actual task. Remember a task can be very short - three or four minutes.
	
	• Reflect also on whether the learning outcome reported by the students corresponded to the aim in the lesson plan.

A communic- ative activity for two tutors!	Tutor A	Tutor B
	• Find a colleague. • Ask your colleague to suggest a topic. • Discuss how a communicative activity can be made for it.	• Find a colleague. • Ask your colleague to suggest a topic. • Discuss how a communicative activity can be made for it.

Further reading

Arthur L and S Hurd, *The adult language learner* (CILT, 1992)

Littlewood W, *Communicative language teaching: an introduction* (CUP, 1981)

Pattison P, *Developing communication skills* (CUP, 1987)

Sidwell D, *Adult learning strategies and approaches: modern language learning* (NIACE, 1987)